Crabapples

Weird Animals

Tammy Everts & Bobbie Kalman

Crabtree Publishing Company

Crabapples

created by Bobbie Kalman

for John, the weirdest animal I know

Editor-in-Chief
Bobbie Kalman

Writing team
Tammy Everts
Bobbie Kalman

Managing editor
Lynda Hale

Editors
David Schimpky
Petrina Gentile
Lynda Hale

Computer design
Lynda Hale
David Schimpky

Color separations and film
Dot 'n Line Image Inc.

Printer
Worzalla Publishing Company

Illustrations
Barb Bedell

Special thanks to Kristen Sacco, who provided information for the chapter on manatees.

Photographs
Ernest Braun: page 23
Dave B. Fleetham/Visuals
  Unlimited: page 17
Mary Mason: page 22
Galen Rowell/Mountain Light
  Photography: page 11
Kjell B. Sandved/Visuals
  Unlimited: pages 5 (bottom), 10
Science VU/Visuals Unlimited:
  page 8 (top)
Tom Stack & Associates:
  D. Holden Bailey: page 26
  John Cancalosi: page 5 (top)
  Dave B. Fleetham: page 4
  Manfred Gottschalk:
    pages 8-9 (bottom)
  Thomas Kitchin: page 15

Tom Stack & Associates cont'd:
  Joe McDonald: page 14 (top)
  Gary Milburn:
    pages 14 (bottom), 18
  M. Timothy O'Keefe: page 27
  Brian Parker: title page,
    pages 20 (top), 30
  Rod Planck: cover, pages 24-25
  Ed Robinson: page 16
  Kevin Schafer & Martha Hill:
    page 20 (bottom)
  Wendy Shattil & Bob Rozinski:
    page 19
  Larry Tackett: page 12
  Roy Toft: page 21
  Barbara von Hoffman: page 13
  Dave Watts: pages 6-7, 28, 29

Crabtree Publishing Company

350 Fifth Avenue
Suite 3308
New York
N.Y. 10118

360 York Road, RR 4,
Niagara-on-the-Lake,
Ontario, Canada
L0S 1J0

73 Lime Walk
Headington
Oxford OX3 7AD
United Kingdom

Cataloging in Publication Data
Everts, Tammy, 1970-
  Weird animals

(Crabapples)
Includes index.

ISBN 0-86505-617-X (library bound) ISBN 0-86505-717-6 (pbk.)
This book looks at the bodies, diets, and habits of unusual birds, reptiles, mammals, and fish.

1. Animals - Juvenile literature. I. Kalman, Bobbie, 1947-
II.Title. III. Series: Kalman, Bobbie, 1947-   . Crabapples.

QL49.E84 1995   j591   LC 94-34784
                                              CIP

What is in this book?

What is a weird animal?

What are "weird animals?" Why are they "weird?" "Weird" is a word that means eerie, odd, or unusual. It can also describe something that is hard to explain.

Some of the animals in this book have unusual bodies. Others have strange diets. A few have habits that people find hard to understand.

In the animal world, everything has a purpose—even things about animals that might seem weird to people. For example, a giraffe's long neck helps it eat leaves from tall trees.

Many weird animals are **endangered**. This means that they are in danger of disappearing from the wild. Often, weird animals can only live in one special environment. If their home changes or is destroyed, these animals die because they cannot find a new home.

Platypus

The platypus resembles several animals. It has fur and a tail like that of a beaver, but its bill and webbed feet are like those of a duck. The platypus is about the size of a rabbit. Although it lays eggs like a bird, it is a **mammal**. A platypus mother feeds her babies with milk from her body.

The platypus spends a lot of time in the water. It paddles with its front feet and steers with its hind feet. It swims near the bottom of lakes and rivers. With its wide, flat bill, the platypus scoops through sand to dig up the worms and small water animals that it eats.

The male platypus has sharp spurs and venom sacs on its back feet. It can scratch its enemies and poison them with venom.

6

Komodo dragon

The island of Komodo is part of a country called Indonesia. This island is home to an animal called the Komodo dragon. The Komodo dragon is not really a dragon, but it does look like a creature from a fairy tale. It has scaly skin and a long tail. The Komodo dragon is the largest lizard in the world. It can grow up to four meters (13 feet) long. That is longer than a car!

Most lizards eat insects and plants, but the Komodo dragon hunts and kills animals. It has bad-smelling breath because it also eats dead animals! A Komodo dragon can swallow some animals in a single gulp.

A Komodo dragon is afraid of only one animal—a bigger Komodo dragon. Baby dragons climb trees to escape from hungry adult dragons that might eat them. When the young dragons are large enough to defend themselves, they live on the ground.

a baby Komodo dragon

9

Penguin

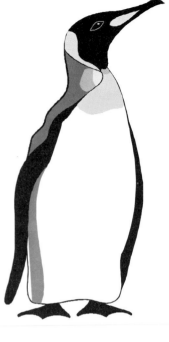

Although penguins are birds, they cannot fly in the air as most birds can. Instead, they "fly" under water. A penguin's wings are actually flippers that help the penguin swim gracefully. Its feathers are not like those of other birds. They are tiny and grow close together. They keep the penguin warm in cold water.

A penguin may look as if it is wearing a suit, but its colors are not meant to be fashionable. Its black back hides the penguin from seals that may be swimming above it in the dark water. If a seal is swimming below the penguin, the white stomach is hard to see against the sunlight shining into the water.

Lemur

A lemur looks a little like a raccoon, but it is a member of the **primate** family. Monkeys, apes, and people are also primates. Long ago, lemurs lived in many parts of the world. Now, only a few are left on Madagascar, an island in the Indian Ocean.

Lemurs are shy, gentle mammals that spend most of their time in trees. They eat fruit and insects. Lemurs live in large family groups. The females are in charge.

Bat

Most insects and birds can fly, but there is only one mammal that flies. It is the bat. The bat has a furry body like that of a mouse. Its wings are covered with leathery skin.

During the day, groups of bats hang upside-down and sleep. At night, they fly around and hunt for food. Most bats eat insects or fruit. Bats that eat insects are important to the environment. They help keep the number of harmful insects under control.

There are many different kinds of bats, but the vampire bat on the left is one of the weirdest. It bites animals such as cows, horses, and pigs and feeds on their blood.

Octopus

What animal has eight arms and no legs? The octopus does! An octopus's "arms" are called **tentacles**. The bottom of each tentacle has rows of suckers that look like suction cups. The octopus uses its tentacles and suckers to crawl along the ocean floor. Suckers are also useful for holding the crabs and lobsters the octopus eats.

An octopus has a special sac inside its body. When it senses danger, it squirts a cloud of black ink from its sac. The ink makes it difficult for an enemy to see, giving the octopus time to escape. Long ago, people used this ink for writing.

An octopus is a very intelligent animal. It has a good memory. It can open jars and perform tricks. Keeping an octopus in a tank is difficult because the octopus can figure out how to escape.

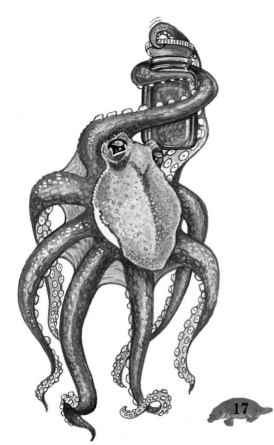

Anteater

The anteater is a mammal with a special body that helps it find and eat ants. Its short legs keep the anteater close to the ground, where it can smell and hear insects. When the anteater finds a nest of ants or termites, it rips the nest apart with its long, sharp claws.

The anteater puts its long snout into a hole and pokes out its sticky, wormlike tongue. It then pulls its tongue—insects and all—into its mouth. Sharp hooks on the tongue, called **barbs**, keep insects from escaping.

an anteater's tongue

Some small anteaters have a **prehensile** tail. Something that is prehensile can wrap around objects and hold on tightly. An anteater wraps its tail around branches to hold itself up in a tree.

Orangutan

The orangutan is an endangered ape that lives in the rain forest. People who live in the rain forest gave the orangutan its name. It means "old man of the forest."

The orangutan has long, strong arms. They are useful for climbing and swinging through trees.

Male orangutans have big cheeks and chins called **blinkers**. Blinkers are stored-up fat that can be used by the orangutan's body when food is hard to find. When a male meets another male, the large blinkers make him look bigger and scarier to the other orangutan.

Bonobo

Some people call bonobos "pygmy chimpanzees" because they look like small chimpanzees. Bonobos and chimpanzees are related, but they are different in many ways.

Chimpanzees often fight over food, but bonobos are peaceful and share their meals. In a chimpanzee family, the males are the leaders. In a bonobo family, the females are more powerful.

Bonobos sometimes walk upright on their back legs. From far away, they look like small people.

bonobo

chimpanzee

21

Blue-footed booby

The booby is a large bird that lives in tropical areas near the ocean. The blue-footed booby is named for its unusual bright blue feet.

The blue-footed booby has an energetic **mating dance**. When a male wants to get a female's attention, he shows off his fabulous feet with a high-stepping march. At the end of the dance, both boobies stand chest to chest with their beaks pointing to the sky.

The blue-footed booby keeps its eggs warm by standing on them. It has very warm feet. To stay warm, baby boobies stand on the feet of their parents. Do baby boobies also have blue booties?

Star-nosed mole

The star-nosed mole is a small furry mammal with sharp teeth, soft fur, and short legs. Its huge front paws have two purposes—digging and swimming. Like other moles, the star-nosed mole digs underground tunnels. This weird mole, however, spends most of its time swimming in streams and ponds.

The star-nosed mole's nose looks like a pink star. There are 22 very sensitive **feelers** at the tip of the snout. The mole is almost blind. To find food, it uses its feelers like fingers. When the star-nosed mole swims under water, it covers its nostrils with twenty of its feelers. The other two are left poking out to help the mole feel its way.

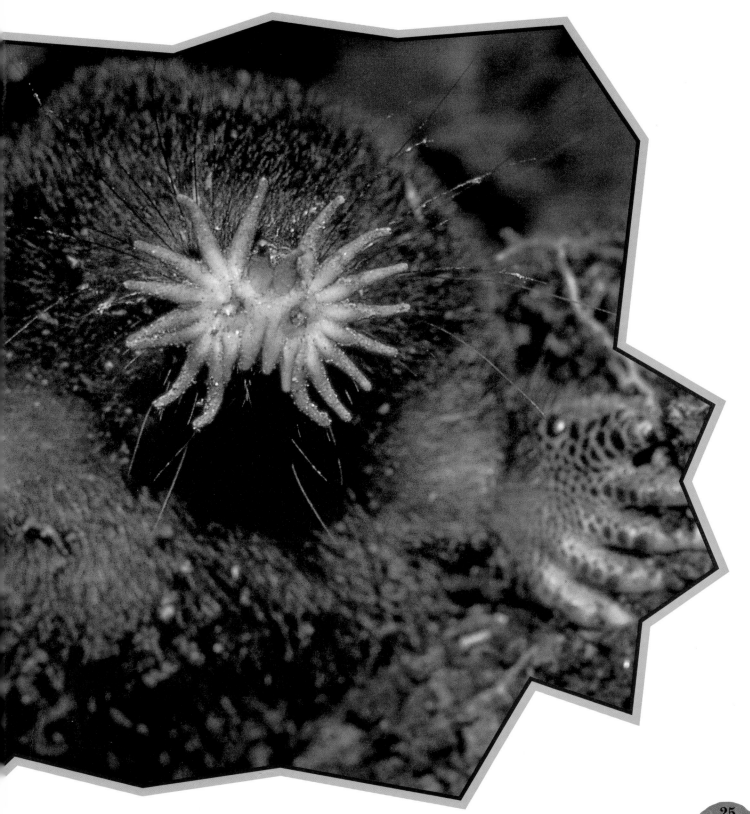

Manatee

Sailors once thought that manatees were mermaids. Today, some people call manatees "sea cows," but the manatee is not a cow. It is a large, friendly mammal that lives in fresh or salt water in Florida, the Caribbean, and the northern coast of South America.

Manatees often travel together in small groups. Mothers and babies sometimes swim with their flippers linked, as if they were holding hands. Sometimes mother manatees cradle their babies in their flippers.

Baby manatees are born under water. Newborn babies are one meter (three feet) long. They can weigh up to 30 kilograms (70 pounds).

Manatees are **herbivores**, which means that they eat plants. Manatees eat water plants that could clog rivers and canals.

Manatees are endangered. Motorboats that speed along rivers are the greatest danger to their lives. Many manatees are injured or killed by boat propellers.

Animals with pockets

How would you like to live in a pocket? Most female **marsupials** carry their babies in a special pouch on their body. The babies are tiny, hairless, and blind when they are born, but they climb up their mother's body to her pouch. The babies sleep and drink milk from the mother's nipples inside the pouch.

nipple

a newborn kangaroo

Kangaroo babies are called **joeys**. A joey lives in its mother's pouch for six months to a year. When the joey is older, it hops along beside its mother. When it is frightened, it jumps back into her pouch. The pademelon on the left is a small member of the kangaroo family.

There are many different types of opossum. A female opossum has up to 25 babies at once. The babies stay hidden in their mother's pouch until they are old enough to stay on her back. They use their tiny paws to cling tightly to her fur.

The mouse opossum in this picture is unusual—even for an opossum! The mother does not have a pouch. For three weeks, each baby holds a nipple in its mouth and hangs.

A female koala has just one baby in her pouch. The baby lives in the pouch for six months. After that, the baby rides on its mother's back.

Kangaroos, opossums, koalas, and most other marsupials live in Australia and New Guinea. Some opossums live in North America as well.

Mudskipper

Most fish die if they are out of water, but not the mudskipper! This unusual fish sometimes leaves the water to hunt for crabs, worms, and other small animals. It walks on land using its flippers as feet. Some mudskippers even climb trees.

The mudskipper survives out of water by carrying its own water supply. It stores the water in special sacs inside its body. These sacs are called **gill chambers**.

Words to know

blinkers The fat cheeks and chin of a male orangutan

endangered Describing a type of plant or animal that is nearly extinct

gill chamber The sac in a mudskipper's body used for storing water

herbivore An animal that eats only plants

mammal A warm-blooded animal with a backbone and hair or fur

marsupial A family of animals in which the female carries her babies in a pouch on her body

mating dance The special movements made by an animal to attract a mate

prehensile Describing a limb that can wrap around objects

primate A family of animals that includes monkeys, apes, and people

rain forest A thick forest that receives a great deal of rain

sac A pouch in an animal's body that often contains a liquid

tentacle A long flexible limb used for feeling, grasping, and moving

venom A type of poison

Index

What is in the picture?

Here is more information about the photographs in this book.

1 2 3 4 5 6 7 8 9 0 Printed in USA 4 3 2 1 0 9 8 7 6 5